Character Education

Friendliness

by Lucia Raatma

Consultant:
Madonna Murphy, Ph.D.
Associate Professor of Education
University of St. Francis, Joliet, Illinois
Author, *Character Education in America's Blue Ribbon Schools*

Bridgestone Books
an imprint of Capstone Press
Mankato, Minnesota

W9-CKC-693

Bridgestone Books are published by Capstone Press
151 Good Counsel Drive, P.O. Box 669, Mankato, Minnesota 56002
http://www.capstone-press.com

Library of Congress Cataloging-in-Publication Data
Raatma, Lucia.
    Friendliness/by Lucia Raatma.
      p. cm.—(Character education)
    Includes bibliographical references and index.
    Summary: Describes friendliness as the virtue of being kind and helpful and
suggests ways in which friendliness can be shown.
    ISBN 0-7368-0368-8
    1. Friendship—Juvenile literature. [1. Friendship. 2. Kindness.
3. Helpfulness.] I. Title. II. Series.
BJ1533.F8R33   2000
177'.62—dc21
                                                              99-31308
                                                              CIP

Editorial Credits
Christy Steele, editor; Heather Kindseth, cover designer and illustrator;
   Kimberly Danger, photo researcher

Photo Credits
Corbis, 18
David F. Clobes, 6
International Stock/Dusty Willison, cover
Photo Network/Jeff Greenberg, 4
Photri-Microstock/Bachmann, 8
Shaffer Photography/James L. Shaffer, 12, 20
Unicorn Stock Photos/Robert W. Ginn, 14; Chris Boylan, 16
Visuals Unlimited/Mark E. Gibson, 10

2 3 4 5 6 06 05 04 03 02 01

Table of Contents

Friendliness

Friendliness means being kind and helpful. Friendly people smile and greet others. They include everyone in their activities. Friendly people make others feel better about themselves. People will enjoy spending time with you if you are friendly.

Being Friendly with Yourself

You can practice friendliness with yourself. Be nice to yourself if you make mistakes. Understand that you are a special person. Focus on your good qualities. You may be able to tell funny jokes. You may be a good listener.

qualities
the special features someone has

Being Friendly at Home

Being friendly with your family will help everyone get along. You can share your ideas with your mother. You can play a game with your older sister. You can make your little brother laugh. You may find that your best friends live at home.

Being Friendly to Your Friends

Being friendly will help you make and keep friends. Practicing friendliness will make your friends feel comfortable with you. You can share ideas and feelings with one another. You can play games together and share your toys.

comfortable
feeling relaxed; not worried

Friendliness at School

You can show friendliness at school in many ways. You can save a seat for someone at lunch. You can read a book with a friend. You can ask a new classmate to play with you and your friends. Friendly people make school more fun.

Helping Others

Helping others is a good way to show friendliness. You can help decorate for a friend's birthday party. Your brother might need your help to clean his room. Washing your family's car helps your parents. You can rake leaves for your grandparents.

Friendliness in Your Community

You can practice friendliness in your community. You can use people's names when you greet them. You can help a neighbor shovel snow. Tell your neighbors if you see strangers around their homes. Friendly people make communities safe and fun.

"I never met a man I didn't like."
—Favorite saying of Will Rogers

Friendly Will Rogers

Will Rogers was a famous cowboy. He starred in movies, plays, and radio shows. Will treated all people with respect and friendliness. He greeted everyone he met with a big smile. He told jokes to cheer up people. Will's friendliness made him a national hero.

Friendliness and You

Friendliness is about thinking of other people. Being nice and helpful sometimes is hard. But you will feel good about yourself if you help others. People will appreciate your company. You will make friends. Good friends will help you when you have problems.

appreciate
to enjoy or value someone or something

Hands On: Remembering Birthdays

Special days such as birthdays are important to people. You can show friendliness by remembering someone's special day.

What You Need
Paper
Scissors
A hat

What You Do
1. Write your name and birthday on the paper. Pass the paper around the class. Ask everyone to write down their name and birthday on the paper.
2. Ask your teacher to cut the list into pieces. Each piece will have a name and a birthday.
3. Put the pieces in a hat.
4. Have each person in your class draw a name from the hat.
5. Ask your classmates to remember the birthday they drew.

Classmates can remember that person's birthday by sending a card. Or they can plan a birthday party. Ask your teacher to help you with birthday party plans.

Words to Know

appreciate (uh-PREE-shee-ate)—to enjoy or value someone or something

comfortable (KUHM-fur-tuh-buhl)—feeling relaxed; not worried

focus (FOH-kuhss)—to pay attention to something or someone

quality (KWAHL-uh-tee)—a special feature of someone or something

Read More

Baxter, Nicola. *Friends.* Toppers. Chicago: Children's Press, 1996.
Ross, Dave. *A Book of Friends.* New York: HarperCollins, 1999.
Scott, Elaine. *Friends.* New York: Atheneum Books, 2000.
Suben, Eric. *Friendship.* Doing the Right Thing. Vero Beach, Fla.: Rourke, 1999.

Internet Sites

Adventures from the Book of Virtues Home Page
http://www.pbs.org/adventures
Character Counts! The Six Pillars of Character
http://charactercounts.org/defsix.htm
Profiles of Giraffe Heroes
http://www.giraffe.org/heroes.html

Index